Book Market

HEMANTA SAIKIA

&

EMI KALITA

DEDICATION

To my Parents and other family members.

CONTENTS

ACKNOWLEDGMENTS

I would also like to give my special thanks to my family whose patient love enabled me to complete this work. I extend due respect and gratitude to all those who helps and co-operations will be valuable and precious for all time to come before me.

1 INTRODUCTION

Books are the major factor in the enlightening life of a nation; however, not very much attention has been dedicated to the book market in cultural economics. Historically, books have been the major means of communication of new thoughts in times where the majority of the people had little opportunity to go to the theatre and electronic leisure was not yet invented. The influence of authors has certainly been recognized, frequently by kings and almost habitually by dictators trying to combat treacherous ideas. As always, the book market is determined by the forces of supply and demand, and in each period a great many new books, or titles, are introduced, priced, and sold. Let us start with the supply side. In each period, the publishers will be offered a number of manuscripts from national authors. These manuscripts may come to the publishers exogenously or they may have been commissioned, but the origin of the manuscript, while very important to the individual author and for the individual contract, is probably not very important for the book market. Very little is solidly known about the number of manuscripts offered to the publishers, or how many manuscripts those are rejected and possibly reoffered to another publisher

Figure: 1 Traditional Book Publishing Process

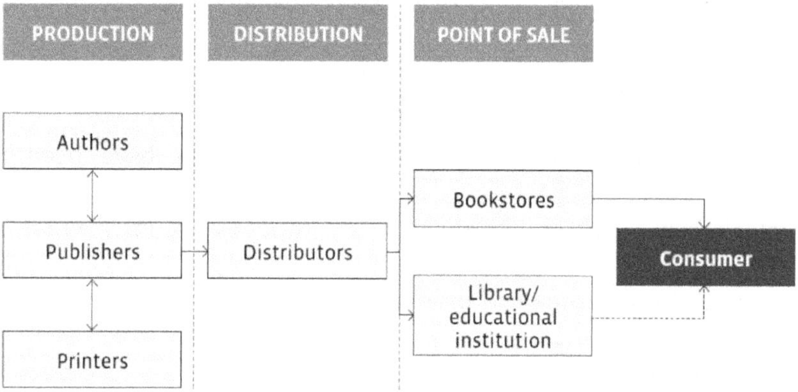

Books are the major factor in the intellectual development of a nation. Historically, books have been the major means of communication of new thoughts in times where the majority of the people had little opportunity to go to the theatre and electronic entertainment was not yet invented. The influence of authors has certainly been recognized, frequently by kings and almost invariably by dictators. The traditional book distribution system was simple and authors and publishers are hub of production system which is distributed by distributors and points of sale are bookstores and libraries. However, with the development of science and technology especially the electronic media, the whole picture has changed and electronic books distributed by thousands of consumers communication systems has occupied a key role in distribution of book. The production structure and cost production of these books are totally different from the traditional print book system. Books eventually will become secondary tools in academia, usurped by electronic media. Textbooks, will be replaced by multimedia instructional technologies incorporating pictures, symbols and video clips. Change will come not because the new forms are superior to traditional face-to-face teaching, but rather because they can be provided for significantly lower costs. Further, commercial firms will be the primary providers of the new electronic curriculum, not today's nonprofit colleges and universities. Noam reviews the effects of these changes on the publishing industry and the higher education marketplace.

In the global scenario, the digital world has shifted the static picture of book market to a dynamic one. Now a day, publishers, internet bookstores, and companies that manufacture e-Readers have high expectations for the digital future of the book industry. A new generation of e-Readers may, at last, achieve the long-awaited breakthrough that lures consumers away from paper and ink. In the United States, Amazon has revolutionized the market by producing an e-reader that is easy to use and making it easy for customers to purchase a wide variety of books at competitive prices. While some people herald the advent of digital reader technology as an opportunity to open new target markets and create customers, others mourn the end of traditional books and doubt the industry will be able to retain control over pricing and content.

2 CONSUMER CONFIDENCE

Before discussing the global marketing scenario, it is very much required to know the term global consumer confidence. Consumer confidence is an economic indicator which measures the degree of optimism that consumers feel about the overall state of the economy and their personal financial situation. How confident people feel about stability of their incomes determines their spending activity and therefore serves as one of the key indicators for the overall shape of the economy. In essence, if the economy expands causing consumer confidence to be higher, consumers will be making more purchases and vice versa. The Nielsen Global Survey of Consumer Confidence and Spending Intentions, established in 2005, tracks consumer confidence, major concerns and spending intentions among more than 28,000 Internet consumers in 56 countries. Consumer confidence levels above and below a baseline of 100 indicate degrees of optimism and pessimism.

Nielsen Global Consumer Confidence Index—56 countries, three month trend

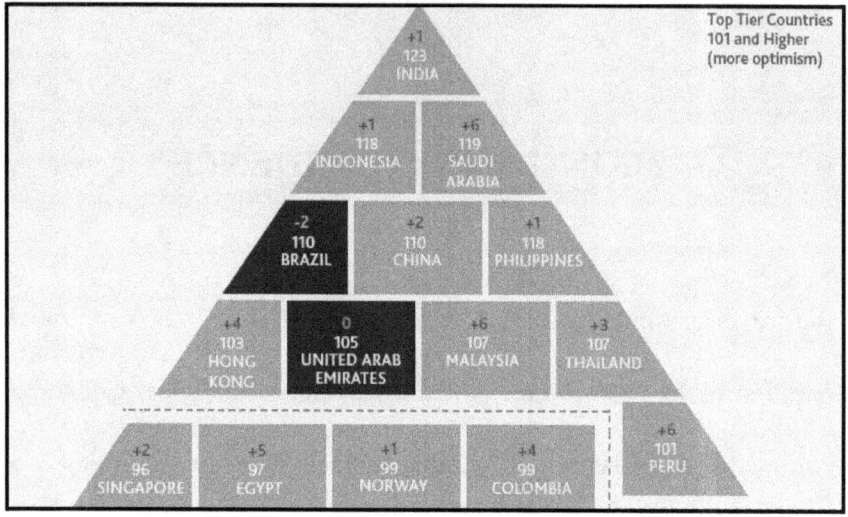

(Index levels above and below 100 indicate degrees of optimism/pessimism)

The global scenario of Nielsen Global Consumer Confidence Index 2012 represents an optimistic picture. The South Asian countries are performing better than the western countries in terms of Nielsen Global Consumer Confidence Index which is mainly due to little impact of global recession on South Asian countries. India is at the top of the countries in terms of Global Consumer Confidence Index 2012 (index value 123). Although the sentiment of rising inflation combined with other economic and personal pressures have taken a toll on consumer confidence, the Indian consumer seems to have reconciled with the challenges. In a typically resilient fashion, they have adopted various strategies to counter inflation through a much keener effort to seek better deals at the point of sale and by timing bigger ticket purchases. The relevance of a consumer confidence index for a country like India is evident from the fact that Consumption Expenditure accounts for over 60% of India's GDP. Therefore, South Asian countries are opening avenues for investment in consumer goods as well as global book marketing.

3. INTERNATIONAL BOOK MARKETS

Attitudes toward eBooks and e-Readers seem to differ on each side of the Atlantic. In the United States, publishers appear amenable to eBooks because they generally offer lower costs and higher margins than print. An eBook publisher does not incur inventory return costs that are typically associated with traditional print channels. In Europe, publishers seem more likely to view digital publishing as a step backward for their companies – a necessary evil, so to speak – that represents more risks than opportunities. Therefore, European publishers are more likely to express doubts about digital transformation in the industry, and act slowly out of fear of high costs and the possibility of losing sales of print books.

However, the progress toward a digital publishing industry

can only move forward. This is most obvious with the developments in the United States, where eBooks accounted for about 3% of the overall market at the end of 2009 and will account for 7% in 2010 which is only the beginning: Driven by the improvement of reading devices with integrated online stores, an extensive range of electronic books, and an aggressive price policy of online retailers such as Amazon, eBook revenue continues to expand. The market is being further stimulated by multifunction devices such as Apple's iPad, and it has already proved lucrative for publishers, whose initial investments are paying off because of higher margins for eBooks. There is no doubt that the same trends that spurred the adoption of eBooks and eReaders in the United States are having a similar effect in other countries as well. Technical development and sophistication of reading devices that provide an experience similar to that of reading an actual book. The increasing penetration of the Internet in all areas of life is significantly changing reading patterns and reading behavior. The increasing extent to which consumers are open to new technological trends, for which in particular the availability of attractive mobile devices such as smart phones, portable games consoles, and MP3 players are responsible.

With the development of the eBook market the print market declines significantly all over the world.

Print Book Sales Decline across all Markets Broad Sector declines across Markets

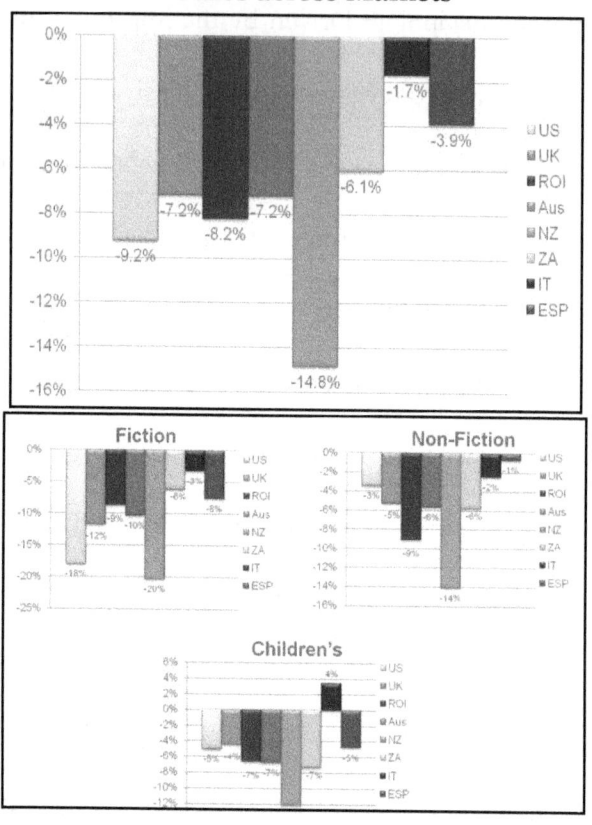

There is a marked decline in the global print Book. The decline of fiction print book is more in Newzeland and USA. Thus, major book markets are experiencing decline in book sales as the global economy and consumer confidence remain fragile. The impact of e-book sales is now having a clear effect on physical book sales in the US and UK, with this effect likely to increase in these markets and begins to be felt in other territories. The rapid growth of eBook sales seems, "anecdotally", to be slowing in the US. However, India is seeing strong growth in book sales, showing that developing economies can hold great opportunities for publishers and booksellers. The online world Split into offline and online sales: offline sales see an increase of 35% and online sales see a massive 178% increase.

4 INDIAN BOOK MARKET

The publishing industry in India is vibrant both in terms of volume and value of production. It is the only country where books are published in more than 20 languages; approximately 90,000 titles are published each year. Out of total publications in India, 31.4 per cent are fictions, 21.4 per cent are children's and remaining 47.3 per cent are non fictions book. According to a Techno pack Advisors report of 2008, the Indian book market is valued at around $2.6 billion and less than one percent of India's $2 billion book industry comes from the online segment. Hence, the internet has a good potential for India's book retail industry.

According to a Techno pack Advisors report of 2008, the Indian book market is valued at around $2.6 billion and less than one percent of India's $2 billion book industry comes from the online segment. Hence, the internet has a good potential for India's book retail industry. Flipkart.com, an Indian online book retailer, sold over 2,000 copies. According to Sachin Bansal, Co-Founder and CEO of Flipkart, the company did well because its main focus was to meet consumer expectations. Flipkart, which was started in 2007 with initial costs of $9,000 and 50,000 titles, made over $4 million in revenue last year. Tt raised $8-10 million from New York-based venture capital fund Tiger Global Management. Flipkart isn't the only player in India's online bookstore arena who is hopeful in this regard. Infibeam, a Gujarat-based online book retailer, has also recorded $20 million revenue target for the year. The list also includes Firstandsecond, Librarywala and Tradusbooks among others who are hopeful of getting a foothold in the market. Online book retailing has some key advantages like potentially infinite shelf space, no real estate costs, an absence of the personnel and infrastructure expenses involved with running a physical store, lower prices and no inter-state taxes. Adding to it, there is easy scalability, which is the best part of it. However, there are some problems too. According to Mahendra Swarup, President, Indian Venture Capital Association, The market should have a level of maturity before e-tailing and e-commerce can take off. The reason behind Swarup's remark may be India's relatively low levels of Internet penetration. According to an I-Cube (Internet in India) study conducted annually by IMRB International and the Internet and Mobile Association of India (IAMAI), India had 52 million active Internet users as of September 2009. But only 10 percent of those users indulge in e-commerce. While most online vendors stock regional language books, those titles usually account for less than one percent of a total stock that averages 6-7 million. But according to observers, more than regional language books, Indian websites are most lacking in user interface and service. Emerging vendors like Infibeam's Mehta and Flipkart's Bansal, realize the importance of customer service; both implemented a "no-questions-asked" return policy on their sites and plan on including user history, reviews and recommendations in the near future.

The Strategist (October 21, 2008) provides estimates of the size of the Indian publishing industry, based on data provided by Technopak Advisors. The Indian publishing market is estimated at Rs 20,000 crore (~ US$ 4.5 Billion) it consists of books, magazines and newspapers. The books market is estimated to be Rs 13,000 crore (~ US$ 2.9 Billion), which is segmented into education and non-education books market.

INDIA TAKES TOP SPOT IN NIELSEN'S GLOBAL CONSUMER CONFIDENCE

India has touched the peak mark in consumer confidence among the 60 countries calculated in Nielsen's Global Survey of Consumer Confidence and Spending Intentions in the second quarter (April-June) of 2014. The country's ranking increased seven index points to 128, surpassing the 123 logged by Indonesia, which previously held the top spot for five consecutive quarters. The Nielsen consumer confidence index measures insights of occupation prospects, personal finances and immediate expenditure intentions. Consumer confidence levels above and below a baseline of 100 indicate degrees of optimism and pessimism, respectively. India's job sentiment improved 20 percentage points from the third quarter of 2013, as 83 percent of Indian consumers said they feel hopeful about future forecast, the survey revealed. According to the Nielsen findings, global consumer confidence increased one index point to 97 in the second quarter, marking the highest level since the first quarter of 2007. This forward momentum comes after a stagnant 2013, when confidence was stubbornly stuck at 94 for three out of four quarters, Nielsen said. Confidence was highest in the Asia-Pacific region, which held steady from the first quarter with a score of 106, whereas North America (103) and Europe (77) reported consumer confidence increases of three and two points, respectively, from the first quarter.

ONLINE BOOK MARKET IN INDIA

The Indian book market is valued at around US$2.6 billion, according to a Technopack Advisors report of 2008. "Less than 1% of [India's] US$2 billion book industry comes from the online segment, so the potential of the Internet is huge. Flipkart made over US$4 million in revenue in 2009. It expects to reach US$20 million by March 2011. The site sells a book a minute. On the releasing day of Dan Brown's novel "The Lost Symbol, in September 2009, Flipkart.com, an Indian online book retailer, sold over 2,000 copies. According to Sachin Bansal, Co-Founder and CEO of Flipkart, the company did well because its main focus was to meet consumer expectations. Flipkart is an Indian e-commerce company headquartered in Bangalore, Karnataka. It was founded by Sachin Bansal and Binny Bansal in 2007. In its initial years, Flipkart focused on online sales of books but it later expanded to electronic goods and a variety of other products. Flipkart offers multiple payment methods like credit card, debit card, net banking, e-gift voucher, and Cash on Delivery. Flipkart, has a initial costs of $9,000 and 50,000 titles, made over $4 million in revenue last year. Earlier this year, it raised $8-10 million from New York-based venture capital fund Tiger Global Management. Flipkart isn't the only player in India's online bookstore arena who is hopeful in this regard. Infibeam, a Gujarat-based online book retailer, has also recorded $20 million revenue target for the year. The list also includes first and second, Librarywala and Tradus books among others who are hopeful of getting a foothold in the market. Online book retailing has some key advantages like potentially infinite shelf space, no real estate costs, an absence of the personnel and infrastructure expenses involved with running a physical store, lower prices and no inter-state taxes. Adding to it, there is easy scalability, which is the best part of it. However, there are some problems too. The market should have a level of maturity before e-tailing and e-commerce can take off. The reason behind remark may be India's relatively low levels of Internet penetration. According to an I-Cube (Internet in India) study conducted annually by IMRB International and the Internet and Mobile Association of India (IAMAI), India had 52 million active Internet users as of September 2009. But only 10 percent of those users indulge in e-commerce. While most online vendors stock regional language books, those titles usually account for less than one percent of a total stock that averages 6-7 million. But according to observers, more than regional language books, Indian websites are most lacking in user interface and service.

NATIONAL BOOK PROMOTION POLICY OF INDIA

Realizing the importance of books, the Ministry of Human Resources and Development (MHRD) has come up with a new draft which aims at making India a knowledge society by promoting the culture of book reading. Known as the National Book Promotion Policy (NBPP), this draft is created with a vision of motivating and facilitating the publication of quality books and their reach to all the readers across the country.

The MHRD had set up a National Book Development Board

after 20 years of independence in 1967 to prepare the guidelines for development of the book industry in a state. However, another body by the name of National Book Development Council (NBDC) was constituted in the year 1983. Thereafter, the Council was reconstituted from time to time. The Union Government decided to revive the NBDC in September, 2008 with a new name National Book Promotion Council (NBPC), to facilitate exchange of views on all major aspects of book promotion. Basically, the new council was formed with a motive of fulfilling the recommendations made by the National Policy of Education, 1986.

The first objective of the NBPP is to have more and better books written on all subjects, for which genuine and capable writers will be encouraged. The council has proposed the organization of workshops to teach the authors about the guidelines and their rights as writers. The publishers will be encouraged to work in a professional manner. They will be given requisite guidance and help to achieve the operational competence. Booksellers and Distributors play a crucial role in reaching out to readers and thus efforts will be made to inculcate the bookshop culture, in addition to the book fair culture. In addition to it, the neighborhood library movement will also be supported because libraries act as local nodal agencies to propagate the cause of the books.

The NBPP has given proper attention to the new media also. It has acknowledged the advances in the digital domain but a proper planning is not formulated till now. The task force will have to come up with a good business plan for the publishers in the digital world. Although, companies like Amazon and Flipkart are doing well as internet book sellers, still we have to go miles to achieve a good readership via internet in India. Thus, a concrete plan is definitely needed in this sector. It seems that the task force has taken the publishing of books on paper more seriously than publishing them on internet. According to WHO, developing countries have almost 70% of the world population of visually impaired people, which makes this segment a big sector. However, India has more than 30 major and many minor languages that divide this section into several small pieces. Now, if the task force wants to cater to all these small factions, it will have to ask the publishers for books in various languages, which will cut short their profit margin. Thus, the task force needs to look into the business part to ensure profit for publishes in this category.

The National Book Promotion Policy also recommends an autonomous National Council/Centre of Children's Literature (NCCL) that will work for the promotion of children's literature. However, one problem arises here. Indian authors don't have much to offer to children and thus we will have to seek assistance from foreign publishers but there are enough reasons to be apprehensive about the foreign publishers and the role of Foreign Direct Investment (FDI) in this sector. Therefore, the task force is required to devise a strategic planning to avoid any sort of unfavorable condition in future. The NBPP also visualizes a society in which books will be available and accessible to everyone and such society was always our dream society but everything depends on the implementation of this policy. A few of the suggestions included: pricing policy on books, Public Private Partnership (PPP) in publishing of text book for school children, focus on access to books by print disabled persons and physically challenged and copies of e-books to be deposited in the public libraries by amending the Delivery of Books and Newspapers Act, 1954. Promotion of neighborhood library system was only one of the suggestions amongst many.

*****

5 INTELLECTUAL PROPERTY RIGHTS AND BOOK PUBLISHING

The entire publishing industry depends on copyright to manage relationships between the relevant stakeholders. The rights and obligations of both the parties need to be clearly defined in order to manage and protect intellectual property (IP) against violation. The publishing contract embodies the relationship between the author and the publisher. Without a functional copyright system, the development of a vibrant national publishing industry would be severely hampered. Piracy is another big issue which is hampering the growth of the industry.

Existing or emerging copyright industries are becoming extremely important as contributors to both national economies and the international economy. In fact, in some Asian economies copyright industries have become the key drivers of development and growth. The publishing industry is one of the core copyright industries, which also include the record, film and games industries. Copyright industries are as attractive as part of an economy, because so many other sectors of the economy are enhanced when there are strong, vibrant copyright industries. For example, there are statistics available about the impact of copyright industries on the economy of Singapore. In monetary terms the core local copyright industries contribute 1.56% of Singapore is GDP, or a turnover of S$10 billion, and employ 38 000 people. This internationalization can be something of a double-edged sword, however. Of the many issues that are currently bringing together the publishing community in India, the issue that has generated one of the most significant responses is the proposed amendments to the country's copyright law. Though there is a clear divide between people for and against it, publishers almost unanimously oppose the amendment.

Many Asian countries are implementing legislation to allow and regulate collective management of copyright. While enforcement of copyright through infringement actions may be necessary to create precedents and to promote a culture of copyright compliance, collective management is desirable for both owners and users of copyright material due to its efficiency. Voluntary systems with legislative backup have been adopted into India, Japan and Malaysia. These systems provide that organizations which undertake collective licensing can apply to administrative arms of government for registration of copyright licensing schemes if they can demonstrate that they represent a significant portion of the rights owners for certain classes of works. Once they are registered, they are in a position to seek to enforce the terms of these collective license.

The first Indian patent laws were first promulgated in 1856. These were modified from time to time. New patent laws were made after the independence in the form of the Indian Patent Act 1970. The Act has now been radically amended to become fully compliant with the provisions of TRIPS. The most recent amendment was made in 2005 which were preceded by the amendments in 2000 and 2003. While the process of bringing out amendments was going on, India became a member of the Paris Convention, Patent Cooperation Treaty and Budapest Treaty. The Copyright Act, 1957 as amended in 1983, 1984, 1992, 1994 and 1999 governs the copyright protection in

India. The total term of protection for literary work is the author's life plus sixty years. For cinematographic films, records, photographs, posthumous publications, anonymous publication, works of government and international agencies the term is 60 years from the beginning of the calendar year following the year in which the work was published.

Copyright gives protection for the expression of an idea and not for the idea itself. For example, many authors write textbooks on physics covering various aspects like mechanics, heat, optics etc. Even though these topics are covered in several books by different authors, each author will have a copyright on the book written by him/her, provided the book is not a copy of some other book published earlier. India is a member of the Berne Convention, an international treaty on copyright. Under this Convention, registration of copyright is not an essential requirement for protecting the right. It would, therefore, mean that the copyright on a work created in India would be automatically and simultaneously protected through copyright in all the member countries of the Berne Convention. The moment an original work is created, the creator starts enjoying the copyright. However, an undisputable record of the date on which a work was created must be kept. When a work is published with the authority of the copyright owner, a notice of copyright may be placed on publicly distributed copies. The use of copyright notice is optional for the protection of literary and artistic works. It is, however, a good idea to incorporate a copyright notice. As violation of copyright is a cognizable offence, the matter can be reported to a police station. It is advised that registration of copyright in India would help in establishing the ownership of the work. The registration can be done at the Office of the Registrar of Copyrights in New Delhi. It is also to be noted that the work is open for public inspection once the copyright is registered. As proposed, the amendment sanctions parallel imports, which allow the import of multiple editions of books into the Indian market, rendering the whole point of territorial rights a bit useless. "If the amendment is passed," Abraham says, "any book published anywhere in the world could be sold [in India], infringing on an exclusive Indian edition — published or imported." He continues: "To understand this, one needs to realize that authors own copyright to their works and then assign publishing rights to different territories, so that the book and readers are best served. Vikram Seth, for example, is published in Britain by Hachette, in the US by

HarperCollins, in Canada by McArthur and by Penguin in India. Each territory is protected by law to best publish the work. Without this legal shield, any of the four editions could infringe on each other.

The amendment remains fervently debated, however. Shamnad Basheer, a lawyer focusing on intellectual property (IP) rights and a faculty member at the National University of Juridical Sciences, Kolkata, offers an opposing view. "Leading IP scholars and economists argue that intellectual property rules are essentially anti-competitive and ought to be tolerated only when there is concrete evidence that their benefits outweigh the harm caused by monopoly rents," he says. "But do we have such countervailing evidence to support a clampdown on parallel imports? Such a restriction is not only likely to harm consumer choice, by leaving access to books in the discretionary hands of a small coterie of publishers; it will also hamper competition and curb the growth of newer and more creative forms of distributorship." Basheer notes that, given the advent of e-publishing, "it is only a matter of time before the firmly etched principle of territoriality begins to yield. If the amendment spurs this business model revolution, it will be so much " better. The amendment has been put on hold for now, but will surely generate significant discussion when next raised.

Meanwhile, publishers in the Subcontinent continue to face mounting problems with piracy, finding this increasingly difficult to tackle. The Publishers Association in the UK, with the support of multinational publishing houses with offices in India, is currently fighting a legal battle to try to contain piracy, but awareness on the issue is relatively low in India. Further, even if controlled within India territory, knockoff books still tend to make their way into Pakistan, Nepal and Bangladesh, stunting the potential of local publishing development throughout the region. Waiting at a traffic signal in any major city of the Subcontinent, one would be amazed at the range of pirated books being offered. Till a few years ago, this would only include international bestsellers such as those by Sidney Sheldon and Jeffrey Archer; but today, they include Ramachandra Guha's historical writings to Jaishree Mishra's novels. Major crackdowns have been initiated by firms and lawyers fighting against piracy, but the source of these books remains a mystery. Another major challenge for the publishing industry — though a potentially massive opportunity in the long term — is the advent of relatively easy access to electronic books. Many publishers are already gearing up for this inevitability; last year, for instance, the Bangalore-based digital publisher E C Media International launched its much-awaited Wink e-book reader. Although it has not met with much success to date, it is clearly a path-breaking initiative, with support for 15 Indian languages. In particular, academic publishers have been the frontrunners in adapting to new technologies and offering content on multiple platforms, not only easing access for students and readers but also giving publishers the opportunity to innovate and develop new content. Such obstacles notwithstanding, one thing is for certain: the publishing industry in India and across the Subcontinent will have to cater to multiple audiences in the coming decades. These will have to include the upwardly mobile middle class, the passionate reader, the new reader and the yet-to-be-converted reader. With the Internet offering hitherto untapped territories and readers, the potential is clearly huge. Publishers in the West are already changing course after learning their first lessons, and publishers here in South Asia can now take advantage of that learning. Moreover, with the world looking at innovations coming from this part of the world, the next step is yet to be taken — and it is likely that this is being conceived of on some computer in Delhi, Dhaka or Karachi.

EXPORT POTENTIAL & PROMOTION OF INDIAN PUBLISHING INDUSTRY

There is a huge export potential for books published in India. High quality books enable India to compete successfully in the International book market. Book Fairs have always been a great attraction among book lovers, publishers, publishing agents, illustrators' and| other aspiring publishing professionals. Book fairs provide a perfect platform for new authors to showcase and promote their titles. India has been a guest of honor at the prestigious Frankfurt Book Fair in both 1986 and 2006, the only country to have been accorded that privilege twice. The passage of these two decades offers an interesting opportunity to examine how Indian publishing has re-positioned itself globally; whereas reporting (however little) on the business aspects of publishing underlines the activity of larger multinational (read: British and American) publishers in India, international platforms such as the Frankfurt and London Book Fair provide a glimpse into the rise of the Indian multinational. The presence of an Indian publisher at an international forum is not just limited to the rights to their books being bought and sold in other languages. There is also a larger assertion of what the Indian publisher has to offer to the international publishing community in terms of new ideas and innovative concepts.

An opposing model has also grown in recent years, of publishers in the Subcontinent purchasing the English-language rights for books written in French, German and other European and African languages. There are a lot of interesting books, as they never make their way into the market, with Indian publishers unable to acquire rights to them. Along with Indian publishers, there is an increasing presence of publishers from Pakistan, Bangladesh and Sri Lanka at international fairs. This clearly reflects the greater importance being accorded to the rising potential of these markets, but also of the growing courage of publishers in the region to try out new ways of expanding their lists and engaging in tie-ups. Libraries need to respond to the growing and diversifying information needs of the end-users. They must become a local gateway to the world's knowledge and information. There is a need for traditional libraries to modernize the existing infrastructure and offer state of the art services.

6. CONCLUSION

Reading books continues to be one of the most popular leisure-time occupations around the world, notwithstanding the increasing use and significance of the internet in our daily lives. The book industry that we know and understand today will continue to thrive, but it will be transformed by eBooks and eReaders. In coming years, printed books will still account for the majority of sales. Technology may change rapidly, but people's habits do not. People will continue to want books to fill their bookshelf, give as gifts, and place on their bedside. But make no mistake – modern reading devices such as the Kindle and iPad mark the beginning of a digital transformation, and the book market has taken its first, irreversible steps into new territory. The different requirements will be fulfilled by different print and digital Medias. Therefore, looking at the above picture Indian book market is expected to be expanded rapidly with the global development of book market.

The Indian publishing industry is growing at an impressive pace and India is one of the few (if at all any) major markets in the world which is still seeing growth in both print and digital publishing. The value of the Indian publishing industry in 2012 is estimated at USD 2 Billion J with an overall growth rate of around 15% as per conservative estimates. A nationwide survey conducted by the National Book Trust of India in 2010 revealed that one-fourth of the youth population, a staggering figure of 83 million, recognize themselves as book readers. India also has about 19.000 publishers although out of those only around 12.400 have ISBN's. It is further estimated that about 90.000 titles are published in India every year which includes books across all genres. The Indian market offers great potential for the European economic market. India ranks second after China as one of the world's most attractive investment destinations. India's potential lies in its excellently trained workforce; it's very young population and a relatively stable government, along with above-average profit margins for foreign firms. Given its strength in terms of its youth population, India has not only has a high potential in the area of education, but also massive purchasing power. Germany already has an outstanding reputation in the fields of education, science and technology. Learning German continues to enjoy great popularity around the country. More than half of the total titles published in India are in Hindi and English, with Hindi constituting about 26% followed by English at 24%.5 India ranks third behind the USA and the UK in the publication of English-language books.

THANKS

www.ingramcontent.com/pod-product-compliance
Lightning Source LLC
Chambersburg PA
CBHW071012180526
45168CB00003B/1393